Contents

Farmer

Some farmers work on huge farms, like this one in New Zealand. The sheep farmer looks after thousands of sheep. He **shears** the sheep and sells their wool.

4

Start Reading AND LISTENING

Jobs People Do

Anita Ganeri

QED Publishing

 QED

First published in the UK in 2005 by
QED Publishing
A Quarto Group company
226 City Road
London EC1V 2TT
www.qed-publishing.co.uk

A Catalogue record for this book is available from the British Library.

ISBN 1 84538 436 9

Written by Anita Ganeri
Designed by Melissa Alaverdy
Editor Hannah Ray
Picture Researcher Nic Dean

Series Consultant Anne Faundez
Publisher Steve Evans
Creative Director Louise Morley
Editorial Manager Jean Coppendale

Printed and bound in China

Picture credits

Key: t = top, b = bottom, m = middle, l = left, r = right

Corbis/Ted Horowitz title page, 13t, 22t, / Paul A. Sauders 4b, /Adam Woolfitt 4t, 22mb, /Jim
Craigmyle 7, 18b, /Tom Stewart 8, 19t, /Jean Woodcock; Reflections Photo Library 11, 19b, /J.
Barry O'Rourke 12, /Reuters 13b, 20t, /Macduff Everton 14/**Getty Images**/Pornchai
Kittiwongsakul/AFP 5, / Taxi 10, 22b/**NASA**/16, 17, 21/**Still Pictures**/Jorgen Shytte 6, 22ml,
/Jose Lobao Tello 9t.

These farmers in Thailand have small
fields where they grow rice to eat.
They plant the rice in the ground.
The rice needs lots of water to grow.

5

Teacher

It is the start of the school day in Africa. The children say "Good morning" to their teacher. Then she takes the **register**.

This teacher in Britain helps the children with their work. She listens to them read and helps them with their writing.

Vet

A vet is like a doctor but he or she looks after animals, instead of people.

If your pet is unwell, you can take it to the vet and he or she will find out what is wrong.

Some vets look after wild animals in a wildlife park. The vets have to be careful because some animals can be very dangerous.

Nurse

Nurses work
in a doctor's
surgery or in
a hospital.
They usually
wear uniforms,
like these.

A nurse helps to
care for people
when they are
feeling ill.

Nurses have lots of jobs to do. They talk to the patients, bring them food, give them their **medicines** and make their beds.

Firefighter

Bee, bah! Bee, bah! A fire engine is speeding along the street, with firefighters on board. The firefighters' job is to put out fires. It is dangerous, dirty work.

The firefighters use **hoses** to put out the flames. Sometimes, a fire spreads very far and fast. Then the firefighters may use airplanes to drop water onto the fire.

How do letters and parcels get to your house? You probably have a post person who brings the post every day. He or she might come on foot, by bicycle or in a van.

But if you lived in a village in the desert in India, you might get a surprise. There, the post arrives by camel!

15

Astronaut

Would you like to be an astronaut?

It's one of the most exciting jobs in the world. It takes years of hard work and training before you can blast off into space.

Astronauts often go for walks in space to do repairs on the space shuttle ... and get a brilliant view of planet Earth!

What do you think?

What do farmers in New Zealand do with the sheeps' wool?

Can you remember what the teacher is helping the children to do?

What does
a vet do when
you take your
pet to see him
or her?

A nurse does lots
of jobs. Can you
name some of them?

How might firefighters put out a fire that's spreading very fast?

Imagine you live in a desert village in India. How might your post arrive?

Before you become
an astronaut, what
will you need to do?

Where does
an astronaut
go for a walk?
Can you
remember?

Hoses – long pipes which squirt out water.

Medicines – tablets and injections to make people feel better.

Register – a list of the names of the children in a class.

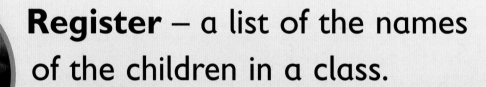

Shear – to cut off a sheep's wool with a special tool.

Surgery – a place where a doctor, nurse or vet works.

Index

Parents' and teachers' notes

- Explain to your child that this book is non-fiction (i.e. that it provides facts and information, rather than tells a story). Point out that the book contains a contents page, a glossary and an index.

- Explain that the reader can look at the contents page to see what the book is about. Point out that the contents page lists all the jobs which appear in the book, in the order in which they appear.

- Together, make a list of other jobs that people do which might appear in another book. Choose one of these jobs and write a page about it.

- Read pages 4–5 about farmers. Talk to your child about other things that farmers grow and other animals that they raise.

- Look at pages 6–7 about teachers. Encourage your child to talk about the sorts of things that his/her own teacher does, such as listening to him/her read.

- Talk to your child about taking a pet to the vet, or going on a trip to a wildife park. Has your child done either of these things? If so, encourage your child to describe his or her visit.

- Choose one of the jobs in the book and pretend that you do that job. Encourage your child to ask you questions about 'your' job. Swap over and let your child imagine that he/she does one of the jobs featured in the book, while you ask the questions.

- Talk to your child about which of the jobs in the book he/she would most like to do. Why would your child like to do that particular job? Talk about the good and bad points about each of the different jobs.

- Leading on from pages 12–13 about firefighters, talk to your child about other people who work in the emergency services, such as police officers and ambulance drivers. What sort of things do these people have to do?

- Encourage your child to imagine what it might be like to be an astronaut. Pretend to be astronauts on a space walk. Together, find out more about the training astronauts do, the equipment they use and the clothes they wear. Help your child to create a fact sheet about astronauts. Can your child draw a picture to accompany your text?